The Poultry Air Fryer Cookbook

The Most Wanted Recipes for Succulent Lean

Meat Meals

Written by

Marion Bartolini

Copyright 2021 © [Marion Bartolini]

Legal & Disclaimer

the application of any of the information provided by this book. This disclaimer applies to any loss, damages or injury caused by the use and application, whether directly or indirectly, of any advice or information presented, whether for breach of contract, tort, negligence, personal injury, criminal intent, or under any other cause of action.

You agree to accept all risks of using the information presented inside this book.

You agree that by continuing to read this book, where appropriate and/or necessary, you shall consult a professional (including but not limited to your doctor, attorney, or financial advisor or such other advisor as needed) before using any of the suggested remedies, techniques, or information in this book.

Table Of Contents

Introduction

Thank you for buying this book!

Please note that since air fryers don't require as much oil as oil frying does, they are generally considered healthier. An air fryer reduces the oil content of food to nearly 80% less than oil frying. It is because the food does not absorb as much oil as with oil frying. However, this difference has led to arguments about the taste of air fried food compared to the oil fried variety. Since oil adds more flavor to fried food as it is being absorbed, it comes as no surprise if an air fried food tastes slightly different from oil fried ones. An excellent example is French fries that may taste a lot different when air fried than the usual oil fried delicacy. <u>Chicken, however, turns out pretty great whether sprinkled with oil or not before air frying.</u>

Moreover, spraying the food with oil before air frying gives it an added crispiness compared to the one that was not sprinkled before air frying. Oil on its own is also one of the essential macronutrients and will come in handy in the right proportion.

There are many heart friendly oils out there, which you can spread over your food before air frying to achieve that fabulous taste. These oils can be used to sprinkle your food before air frying to maintain a healthier diet. However, without a doubt, olive oil, coconut oil and avocado oil are the healthiest cooking oils out there. I recommend you to prefer these choices when cooking.

Enjoy!

Turkey, mushrooms and peas casserole

Preparation Time: 10 minutes

Cooking Time: 30 minutes

Servings: 4

Ingredients:

2 lbs. Turkey breasts; skinless, boneless

1 yellow onion; chopped

1 celery stalk; chopped.

1/2 cup peas

1 cup chicken stock

1 cup cream of mushrooms soup

1 cup bread cubes

Salt and black pepper to the taste

Preparation:

In a pan that fits your air fryer, mix turkey with salt, pepper, onion, celery, peas and stock, introduce in your air fryer and cook at 360 °f, for 15 minutes.

Add bread cubes and cream of mushroom soup; stir toss and cook at 360 °f, for 5 minutes more.

Divide among plates and serve hot.

Nutrition: Calories: 271; Fat: 9; Carbs: 16; Protein: 7

Chicken and black olives sauce

Preparation Time: 10 minutes

Cooking Time: 8 minutes

Servings: 2

Ingredients:

1 chicken breast cut into 4 pieces

2 tbsp. Olive oil

3 garlic cloves; minced

For the sauce:

1 cup black olives; pitted

2 tbsp. Olive oil

1/4 cup parsley; chopped

1 tbsp. Lemon juice

Salt and black pepper to the taste

Preparation:

In your food processor, mix olives with salt, pepper, 2 tbsp. Olive oil, lemon juice and parsley, blend very well and transfer to a bowl.

Season chicken with salt and pepper, rub with the oil and garlic, place in your preheated air fryer and cook at 370 °f, for 8 minutes. Divide chicken on plates, top with olives sauce and serve.

Nutrition: Calories: 270; Fat: 12; Carbs: 23; Protein: 22

Turkey Cakes

Preparation Time: 10 minutes

Cooking Time: 10 minutes

Servings: 4

Ingredients:

3 mushrooms, chopped

1 teaspoon garlic powder

1 teaspoon onion powder

Salt and black pepper to the taste

1 and ¼ pounds turkey meat, ground

Cooking spray

Tomato sauce for serving

Direction:

In your blender, mix mushrooms with salt and pepper, pulse well and transfer to a bowl.

Add turkey, onion powder, garlic powder, salt and pepper, stir and shape cakes out of this mix.

Spray them with cooking spray, transfer them to your air fryer and cook for 10 minutes at 320 degrees F.

Serve.

Nutrition: Calories: 200 Fat: 6g Carbs: 2g Protein: 35g

Tandoori chicken

Preparation time: 30 minutes

Cooking time: 15 minutes

Servings: 2

Ingredients:

For the tandoori chicken:

1/2 chicken, halved

2 cloves garlic, peeled, minced

1/2 tbsp fresh ginger, minced

1/4 cup yogurt (Greek)

1/2 tsp chili powder

1/2 tsp salt or to taste

1/2 tsp turmeric powder

Drops of orange food coloring

1/2 tsp garam masala

Cooking spray or oil for basting

To serve (optional:

Lemon wedges to serve

A handful fresh cilantro, chopped, to garnish

Sliced onions to serve

Directions:

Add garlic, chili, ginger, powder, salt, food coloring, turmeric powder, yogurt, and garam masala into a bowl and mix well.

Marinate the chicken with this mixture. Refrigerate for about 30 minutes.

Place the chicken pieces (without the marinade in the air fryer basket.

Spray a little cooking spray or brush with oil. Flip sides and spray again with cooking spray.

Air fry in a preheated fryer at 400 °f for 12 minutes. Flip sides after 6 minutes of cooking, spraying some more oil over the chicken.

Air fry until the internal temperature of the meat shows 165 °f on a meat cooking thermometer.

Serve with sliced onions and lemon wedges.

Nutrition: Calories: 178 Fat: 6 g Carb: 2 g Protein: 25 g

Baked Thai peanut chicken egg rolls

Preparation time: 10 minutes

Cooking time: 8 minutes

Servings: 2

Ingredients:

2 egg roll wrappers

2 tbsps. Thai peanut sauce

2 green onions, chopped

1/2 cup shredded rotisserie chicken

1 small carrot, very thinly sliced

1/8 red peppers, sliced

Directions:

Place chicken in a bowl. Spread Thai peanut sauce over the chicken.

Place the egg roll wrappers on your countertop. Divide equally—carrot, onion, and bell pepper—and place on the wrappers' bottom third. Divide the chicken and place over the vegetables.

Brush the edges of the wrappers with water. Fold the sides slightly over the filling and then roll the wrappers tightly. Cover with moist paper towels until ready to fry.

Spray the egg rolls all over with cooking spray. Place in the air fryer basket.

Air fry in a preheated fryer at 390 °f for 6–8 minutes or until crisp.

Chop into 2 halves and serve with Thai peanut sauce.

Nutrition: Calories: 235 Fat: 2 g Carb: 17 g Protein: 21 g

Chick fila chicken sandwich

Preparation time: 10 minutes

Cooking time: 14 minutes

Servings: 3

Ingredients:

1 chicken breast, skinless, boneless, half an inch in thickness

1 egg

1/2 cup flour (all-purpose)

1 tbsp potato starch

1/2 tsp sea salt

1/4 tsp garlic powder

1/2 tbsp extra virgin olive oil

2–3 hamburger buns, toasted, buttered

1/4 cup dill pickle juice

1/4 cup milk

1 tbsp powdered sugar

1/2 tsp paprika

Ground pepper as per taste

⅛ tsp ground celery seeds

Dill pickle chips to serve

Cayenne pepper as per taste (optional

Mayonnaise to serve

Directions:

Chop chicken into 2–3 parts.

Add chicken and pickle juice into a Ziplock bag and seal it. Turn the bag a few times so that the chicken is well coated with the pickle juice. Chill for 30–60 minutes.

Add egg and milk to a bowl and whisk well.

Add flour, potato starch, and all the spices in another shallow bowl.

First, dip chicken in the egg mixture. Shake to drop off excess egg.

Next, dredge in the flour mixture. Shake to drop off excess flour. This step is necessary.

Put oil in the air fryer basket. Add the chicken pieces to the air fryer basket. Spray some cooking spray over the chicken.

Air fry in a preheated air fryer at 340 °f for 12 minutes. Flip sides after 6 minutes of cooking, spraying some more oil over the chicken.

Increase the temperature to 400 °f. Cook for 2 minutes. Turn to sides and cook the other side for 2 minutes.

1place the chicken on the bottom half of the burger buns. Drop some mayonnaise over it. Place dill pickle chips and sprinkle cayenne pepper if using and serve.

Nutrition: Calories: 281 Fat: 6 g Carb: 38 g Protein: 15 g

Chicken fried rice

Preparation time: 5 minutes

Cooking time: 20 minutes

Servings: 3

Ingredients:

1/2 cups cold rice

1/2 tbsps. Soy sauce

1 green onion, sliced

3/4 cup frozen vegetables of your choice

1/2 tsp vegetable oil

1/2 tsp sesame oil

Salt as per taste

1/2 tbsp chili sauce (optional

Directions:

Add all of ingredients into a bowl and toss well.

Transfer into the air fryer baking accessory.

Place the baking accessory in the air fryer.

air fry in a preheated fryer at 340 °f for 12–15 minutes. Stir every 5 minutes.

Serve hot.

Nutrition: Calories: 420 Fat: 2 g Carb: 80 g Protein: 15 g

Southwest chicken salad

Preparation time: 20 minutes

Cooking time: 30 minutes

Servings: 2

Ingredients:

For chicken:

1/2 boneless, skinless chicken breasts, thawed

1/2 tbsp avocado oil

1/4 tsp cumin powder

1/8 tsp garlic powder

1 tbsp lime juice (freshly squeezed)

1/4 tsp chili powder

1/8 tsp onion powder

1/8 tsp salt or to taste

For salad:

2 cups green leaf lettuce

Small avocado

1/2 cup black beans, drained, rinsed

1/2 cup corn

1/2 cup halved cherry tomatoes

Southwestern dressing or any other dressing of your choice, as required

Directions:

Add chicken, oil, and lime juice into a bowl. Stir until the chicken is well coated with the mixture.

Add and stir all the spices into a bowl. Sprinkle all over the chicken. Cover it well and place it in the refrigerator for 20–30 minutes.

Discard the marinating mixture and place the chicken in the air fryer basket.

Bake in a preheated air fryer at 400 °f for 25 minutes. Flip sides after about 12–13 minutes of baking. Cook till the temperature of the chicken internally is 165 °f.

Remove chicken from the air fryer and place it on your cutting board. When cool enough to handle, chop or shred the chicken.

Put all salad ingredients into a bowl. Add chicken and toss well. Pour dressing on top and toss well.

Serve.

Nutrition (without dressing: Calories: 271 Fat: 6 g Carb: 21 g Protein: 29 g

Chicken shawarma bowl

Preparation time: 10 minutes

Cooking time: 12–15 minutes

Servings: 2

Ingredients:

For chicken shawarma:

1/2 chicken thighs, skinless, boneless, chopped into bitesize pieces

1/2 tsp kosher salt

1 tsp oregano herbs (dry)

1/2 tsp cumin powder

1/4 tsp ground allspice

1 tbsp vegetable oil

1/2 tsp cinnamon powder

1/2 tsp coriander powder

For the bowl:

3/4 cup halved grape tomatoes

1/2 small English cucumber, sliced

1/2 cup pitted olives

1/2 cup cooked cauliflower rice

1 cup salad greens

Dry roasted chickpeas to garnish (optional)

For the dressing (optional):

1/2 cup Greek yogurt

A pinch oregano

1–2 tbsp. Lime juice

Directions:

Add oregano, salt, and all the spices into a bowl and mix well.

Place chicken in a bowl. Drizzle oil over it. Sprinkle spice mixture over it and toss well.

Set aside at room temperature for 30–60 minutes.

Transfer into the air fryer basket.

Air fry in a preheated air fryer at 350 °f for about 12–15 minutes or until crisp. Shake the basket halfway through frying.

For the dressing, prepare the dressing ingredients into a mixing bowl and whisk well.

To assemble, take 2 serving bowls. Divide salad greens among the bowls. Place cauliflower rice, tomatoes, cucumber, chicken shawarma, and olives in whatever manner you desire.

Drizzle the yogurt dressing on top if desired. Garnish with roasted garbanzo beans if using and serve.

Nutrition: Calories: 313 Fat: 17 g Carb: 12 g Protein: 29 g

Potato chip chicken

Preparation time: 15 minutes

Cooking time: 15 minutes

Servings: 2

Ingredients:

1/2 chicken breasts, thinly sliced

2 ounces potato chips, crushed

1 egg

1/2 tsp all-purpose seasoning (optional)

Directions:

Add cooking spray to the air fryer basket.

Beat egg in a shallow, wide dish.

Place crushed chips on a plate.

First, dip chicken slices in the egg. Shake to drop off excess egg. Next, dredge in chips. Press to adhere and place in the air fryer.

Air fry in a preheated air fryer at 400 °f for 12–15 minutes or until brown and cooked through. Turn the chicken halfway through cooking. The outer covering should be brown and crisp as well.

Nutrition: Calories: 314 Fat: 15 g Carb: 14 g Protein: 28 g

Preparation time: 15 minutes

Cooking time: 12 minutes

Servings: 4

Ingredients:

2 tsp olive oil

6 ounces spinach leaves (small)

4 ounces shredded rotisserie chicken breast

3 ounces shredded mozzarella

1/2 cup minced red onion

2/3 cup marinara sauce

12 ounces fresh, prepared whole-wheat pizza dough

Directions:

Place a non-stick pan over medium high heat. Add oil. When the oil heats, add onion and sauté until translucent.

Mix well spinach and cook until it wilts. Turn the heat off.

Add marinara sauce and chicken and mix well.

Make 8 equal portions of the dough. Shape into balls.

Dust your countertop with some flour. Roll the balls of dough into circles of 6 inches in diameter.

Divide the chicken mixture among the rolled dough and place it on one half of the circle. Close the second half over the filling. Crimp the edges to seal.

Spray calzones with cooking spray and place in the air fryer.

Bake in a preheated air fryer at 350 °f for 12–15 minutes or until golden brown. Turn the calzones halfway through baking.

Cool for a few minutes and serve.

Nutrition: Calories: 348 Fat: 12 g Carb: 44 g Protein: 21 g

Preparation time: 10 minutes

Cooking time: 20 minutes

Servings: 4

Ingredients:

⅓ cup no salt added tomato sauce

2 tablespoons low sodium grainy mustard

2 tablespoons apple cider vinegar

1 tablespoon honey

2 garlic cloves, minced

1 jalapeño pepper, minced

3 tablespoons minced onion

4 (5ounce / 142glowsodium boneless, skinless chicken breasts

Directions:

Press preheat, set the temperature at 370°f (188°c).

Put together the tomato sauce, mustard, cider vinegar, honey, garlic, jalapeño, and onion.

Brush the chicken breasts with some sauce and air fry for 10 minutes.

Remove the air fryer basket and turn the chicken; brush with more sauce. Air fry for 5 minutes more.

Remove the air fryer basket and turn the chicken again; brush with more sauce. Air fry for 3 to 5 minutes more, or until the chicken reaches an internal temperature of 165°f.

Discard any remaining sauce. Serve immediately.

Nutrition: Calories: 209 Fat: 10g Carbs: 0g Protein: 26g

Chicken Manchurian

Preparation time: 10 minutes

Cooking time: 20 minutes

Servings: 2

Ingredients:

1pound boneless, skinless chicken breasts

¼ cup ketchup

1 tablespoon tomato-based chili sauce

1 tablespoon soy sauce

1 tablespoon rice vinegar

2 teaspoons vegetable oil

1 teaspoon hot sauce, such as tabasco

½ teaspoon garlic powder

¼ teaspoon cayenne pepper

2 scallions, thinly sliced

Cooked white rice, for serving

Directions:

Slice the chicken into one inch.

Press preheat and set the temperature at 350°f (177°c.)

In a bowl, combine the chicken, ketchup, chili sauce, soy sauce, vinegar, oil, hot sauce, garlic powder, cayenne, and threequarters of the scallions and toss until evenly coated.

Scrape the chicken and sauce into a metal cake pan and place the pan in the air fryer.

Cook until the chicken is bake and the sauce is reduced to a thick glaze, about 20 minutes, flipping the chicken pieces halfway through.

Remove the pan from the air fryer. Spoon the chicken and sauce over rice and top with the remaining scallions. Serve immediately.

Nutrition: Calories: 352 Fat: 33g Carbs: 12g Protein: 4g

Chicken with pineapple and peach

Preparation time: 10 minutes

Cooking time: 15 minutes

Servings: 4

Ingredients:

1 pound (454 g) low sodium boneless, skinless chicken breasts, cut into 1inch pieces

1 medium red onion, chopped

1 (8ounce / 227gcan pineapple chunks, drained, ¼ cup juice reserved

1 tablespoon peanut oil or safflower oil

1 peach, peeled, pitted, and cubed

1 tablespoon corn-starch

½ teaspoon ground ginger

¼ teaspoon ground allspice

Brown rice, cooked (optional

Directions:

Choose to preheat and set the temperature at 380°f (193°c.

In a medium metal bowl, mix the chicken, red onion, pineapple, and peanut oil. Bake in the air fryer for 9 minutes. Remove and stir.

Add the peach and return the bowl to the air fryer. Bake for 3 minutes more. Remove and stir again.

Mix the pineapple juice, the corn-starch, ginger, and allspice well. Put to the chicken mixture and stir to combine.

Bake for 2 to 3 minutes more or until the chicken reaches an internal temperature of 165°f (74°c) on a meat thermometer, and the sauce is slightly thickened.

Serve immediately with brown rice, if desired.

Nutrition: Calories: 330 Fat: 4g Carbs: 5g Protein: 18g

China spicy turkey thighs

Preparation time: 10 minutes

Cooking time: 25 minutes

Servings: 6

Ingredients:

2 pounds (907 g) turkey thighs

1 teaspoon Chinese five spice powder

¼ teaspoon Sichuan pepper

1 teaspoon pink Himalayan salt

1 tablespoon Chinese rice vinegar

1 tablespoon mustard

1 tablespoon chili sauce

2 tablespoons soy sauce

Cooking spray

Directions:

Press Preheat set the temperature at 360F (182C). Put cooking spray in the air fryer basket.

Rub the turkey thighs with five spice powder, Sichuan pepper, and salt on a clean work surface.

Put the turkey thighs in the preheated air fryer and spritz with cooking spray.

Air fry for 22 minutes or until well browned. Flip the thighs at least three times during the cooking.

Meanwhile, heat the remaining ingredients in a saucepan over medium high heat. Cook for 3 minutes or until the sauce is thickened and reduces to two thirds.

Transfer the thighs onto a plate and baste with sauce before serving.

Nutrition: Calories: 250 Fat: 4g Carbs: 2g Protein: 48g

Coconut chicken meatballs

Preparation time: 10 minutes

Cooking time: 14 minutes

Servings: 4

Ingredients:

1pound (454 g) ground chicken

2 scallions, finely chopped

1 cup chopped fresh cilantro leaves

¼ cup unsweetened shredded coconut

1 tablespoon hoisin sauce

1 tablespoon soy sauce

2 teaspoons sriracha or other hot sauce

1 teaspoon toasted sesame oil

½ teaspoon kosher salt

1 teaspoon black pepper

Directions:

Select preheat, set the temperature at 350°f (177°c).

In a large bowl, gently mix the chicken, scallions, cilantro, coconut, hoisin, soy sauce, sriracha, sesame oil, salt, and pepper until thoroughly combined (the mixture will be wet and sticky.

Place a sheet of parchment paper in the air fryer basket. Using a small scoop or teaspoon, drop rounds of the mixture in a single layer onto the parchment paper.

Air fry for 10 minutes, turning the meatballs halfway through the cooking time. Increase the temperature to 400°f (204°c) and air fry for 4 minutes more to brown the meatballs.

Transfer the meatballs to a serving platter. Repeat with any remaining chicken mixture. Serve.

Nutrition: Calories: 321 Fat: 22g Carbs: 9g Protein: 21g

Garlic soy chicken thighs

Preparation time: 10 minutes

Cooking time: 30 minutes

Servings: 2

Ingredients:

2 tablespoons chicken stock

2 tablespoons reduced sodium soy sauce

1½ tablespoons sugar

garlic cloves, smashed and peeled

2 large scallions, cut into 2 to 3inch batons, plus more, thinly sliced, for garnish

2 bone in, skin on chicken thighs (7 to 8 ounces / 198 to 227 g each)

Directions:

Press "preheat" set the temperature at 375F (191C).

In a metal cake pan, combine the chicken stock, soy sauce, and sugar and stir until the sugar dissolves.

Add the garlic cloves, scallions, and chicken thighs, turning the thighs to coat them in the marinade, then resting them skin side up.

Put the pan in the fryer and bake, flipping the thighs every 5 minutes after the first 10 minutes, until the chicken is cooked through and the marinade is reduced to a sticky glaze over the chicken, about 30 minutes.

Take the pan from the air fryer and serve the chicken thighs warm, with any remaining glaze spooned over the top, and sprinkled with more sliced scallions.

Nutrition: Calories: 250 Fat: 19g Carbs: 2g Protein: 23g

Lettuce chicken tacos with peanut sauce

Preparation time: 10 minutes

Cooking time: 6 minutes

Servings: 4

Ingredients:

1pound (454 g) ground chicken

2 cloves garlic, minced

¼ cup diced onions

¼ teaspoon of sea salt

Cooking spray

Peanut sauce:

¼ cup creamy peanut butter, at room temperature

2 tablespoons tamari

1½ teaspoons hot sauce

2 tablespoons lime juice

2 tablespoons grated fresh ginger

2 tablespoons chicken broth

2 teaspoons sugar

For serving:

2 small heads butter lettuce, leaves separated

Lime slices (optional)

Directions:

Press preheat mode and set the temperature at 350°f (177°c). Spritz a baking pan with cooking spray.

Combine the ground chicken, garlic, and onions in the baking pan, then sprinkle with salt. Use a fork to break the ground chicken and combine them well.

Place the pan in the preheated air fryer. Bake in the preheated air fryer for 5 minutes or until the chicken is lightly browned. Stir them halfway through the cooking time.

Meanwhile, get the ingredients for the sauce and mix well in a small bowl.

Pour the sauce in the pan of chicken, then cook for 1 more minute or until heated through.

Unfold the lettuce leaves on a large serving plate, then divide the chicken mixture on the lettuce leaves. Drizzle with lime juice and serve immediately.

Nutrition: Calories: 287 Fat: 16g Carbs: 21g Protein: 19g

Pomegranate glazed chicken with couscous salad

Preparation time: 25 minutes

Cooking time: 20 minutes

Servings: 4

Ingredients:

3 tablespoons plus 2 teaspoons pomegranate molasses

½ teaspoon ground cinnamon

1 teaspoon minced fresh thyme

Salt and ground black pepper, to taste

2 (12ounce / 340g) bone in split chicken breasts, trimmed

¼ cup chicken broth

¼ cup of water

½ cup couscous

1 tablespoon minced fresh parsley

2 ounces (57 g) cherry tomatoes, quartered

1 scallion, white part minced, green part sliced thin on bias

1 tablespoon extra-virgin olive oil

1ounce (28 g) feta cheese, crumbled

Cooking spray

Directions:

Press "preheat" set the temperature at 350°f (177°c). Spritz the air fryer basket with cooking spray.

Combine 3 tablespoons of pomegranate molasses, cinnamon, thyme, and ⅛ teaspoon of salt in a small bowl. Stir to mix well. Set aside.

Place the chicken breasts in the preheated air fryer, skin side down, and spritz with cooking spray. Sprinkle with salt and ground black pepper.

Air fry for 10 minutes, then brush the chicken with half of the pomegranate molasses mixture and flip. Air fry for 5 more minutes.

Brush the chicken with the remaining pomegranate molasses mixture and flip. Air fry for another 5 minutes or until the chicken breasts' internal temperature reaches at least 165°f (74°c).

Meanwhile, pour the broth and water into a pot and bring to a boil over medium high heat. Add the couscous and sprinkle with salt.

Put cover and let it simmer until the liquid is almost absorbed.

Mix well the remaining ingredients, except for the cheese, with cooked couscous in a large bowl. Scatter with the feta cheese.

When the air frying is complete, remove the chicken from the air fryer and allow it to cool for 10 minutes. Serve with vegetable and couscous salad.

Nutrition: Calories: 496 Fat: 21g Carbs: 48g Protein: 30g

Strawberry glazed turkey

Preparation time: 10 minutes

Cooking time: 37 minutes

Servings: 2

Ingredients:

2 pounds (907 g) turkey breast

1 tablespoon olive oil

Salt and ground black pepper, to taste

1 cup fresh strawberries

Directions:

Choose to preheat, set the temperature at 375°f (191°c).

Rub the turkey bread with olive oil on a clean work surface, then sprinkle with salt and ground black pepper.

Transfer the turkey to the preheated air fryer and air fry for 30 minutes or until the turkey reaches at least 165°f (74°c). Flip the turkey breast halfway through.

Meanwhile, prepare the strawberries in a food processor and pulse until smooth.

When the frying of the turkey is complete spread the puréed strawberries over the turkey and fry for 7 more minutes. Serve immediately.

Nutrition: Calories: 269 Fat: 4g Carbs: 10g Protein: 49g

Thai curry chicken balls

Preparation time: 10 minutes

Cooking time: 10 minutes

Servings: 4

Ingredients:

1pound (454 g) ground chicken

¼ cup chopped fresh cilantro

1 teaspoon chopped fresh mint

1 tablespoon fresh lime juice

1 tablespoon Thai red, green, or yellow curry paste

1 tablespoon fish sauce

2 garlic cloves, minced

2 teaspoons minced fresh ginger

½ teaspoon kosher salt

½ teaspoon black pepper

¼ teaspoon red pepper flakes

Directions:

Press "preheat" set the temperature at 400°f (204°c).

In a large bowl, gently mix the ground chicken, cilantro, mint, lime juice, curry paste, fish sauce, garlic, ginger, salt, black pepper, and red pepper flakes until thoroughly combined.

Form the mixture into 16 meatballs.

Set out the meatballs in a single layer in the air fryer basket. Air fry for 10 minutes, turning the meatballs halfway through the cooking time. Serve immediately.

Nutrition: Calories: 300 Fat: 20g Carbs: 16g Protein: 21g

Chicken pasta

Preparation time: 10 minutes

Cooking time: 15 minutes

Servings: 4

Ingredients:

1 lb. Bitesize chicken breasts, boneless and skinless

1 tbsp garlic, minced

2 bell peppers, seeded and diced

2 tbsp olive oil

1 onion, diced

1 cup chicken stock

3 tbsp fajita seasoning

8 oz penne pasta, dry

7 oz can tomato

Directions:

Add olive oil and set pot on sauté mode.

Add chicken and half fajita seasoning in the pot and sauté chicken for 35 minutes.

Add garlic, bell pepper, onions, and remaining fajitas seasoning and sauté for 2 minutes.

Add tomatoes, stock, and pasta and stir well.

Seal the pot with a pressure-cooking lid and cook on high for 6 minutes.

Once done, release pressure using a quick release. Remove lid.

Set pot on sauté mode and cook for 12 minutes. Serve and enjoy.

Nutrition: Calories 462 Fat 30g Carbs 14g Protein 37g

Sweet & tangy tamarind chicken

Preparation time: 10 minutes

Cooking time: 15 minutes

Servings: 4

Ingredients:

2 lbs. Chicken breasts, skinless, boneless, and cut into pieces

1 tbsp ketchup

1 tbsp vinegar

2 tbsp ginger, grated

1 garlic clove, minced

3 tbsp olive oil

1 tbsp arrowroot powder

1/2 cup tamarind paste

2 tbsp brown sugar

1 tsp salt

Directions:

Add oil into the inner pot and set on sauté mode.

Add ginger and garlic and sauté for 30 seconds.

Add chicken and sauté for 4 minutes.

Mix the tamarind paste, brown sugar, ketchup, vinegar, and salt and pour over chicken and stir well.

Seal the pot with a pressure-cooking lid and cook on high for 8 minutes.

Once done, release pressure using a quick release. Remove lid.

Get small bowl and put arrowroot powder with 2 tbsp water, then pour it into the pot.

Set pot on sauté mode and cook chicken for 12 minutes. Serve and enjoy.

Nutrition: Calories 132 Fat 2g Carbs 35g Protein 22g

Tasty butter chicken

Preparation time: 10 minutes

Cooking time: 8 minutes

Servings: 6

Ingredients:

3 lbs. Chicken breasts, boneless, skinless, and cut into cubes

1/2 cup butter, cut into cubes

2 tbsp tomato paste

1 tsp turmeric powder

2 tbsp garam masala

1 tbsp ginger paste

1 tbsp garlic paste

1 onion, diced

1/4 cup fresh cilantro, chopped

1/2 cup heavy cream

1 1/4 cup tomato sauce

2/3 cup chicken stock

1 1/2 tsp olive oil

1 tsp kosher salt

Directions:

Add 3 tbsp butter and oil in the inner pot of instant pot duo crisp and set pot on sauté mode.

Add garlic paste and onion and sauté for a minute.

Add chicken, tomato sauce, stock, tomato paste, turmeric, garam masala, ginger paste, salt, and stir to combine.

Seal the pot with a pressure-cooking lid and cook on high for 5 minutes.

Once done, release pressure using a quick release. Remove lid.

Set pot on sauté mode. Add remaining butter and heavy cream and cook for 2 minutes.

Stir well and serve.

Nutrition: Calories 643 Fat 33 g Carbs 2 g Protein 64 g

Preparation time: 10 minutes

Cooking time: 50 minutes

Servings: 4

Ingredients:

1 1/2 lbs. Chicken thighs, skinless and boneless

2 tbsp Dijon mustard

1/4 cup French mustard

4 tbsp maple syrup

2 tsp olive oil

Directions:

In a large bowl, mix maple syrup, olive oil, Dijon mustard, and French mustard.

Add chicken to the bowl and mix until chicken is well coated.

Transfer chicken into the instant pot air fryer basket and place basket in the pot.

Seal the pot with an air fryer lid, select bake mode, and cook at 375 f for 50 minutes.

Serve and enjoy.

Nutrition: Calories 112 Fat 5g Carbs 3g Protein 18g

Mustard chicken

Preparation time: 10 minutes

Cooking time: 20 minutes

Servings: 4

Ingredients:

1 lbs. Chicken tenders

1 garlic clove, minced

1/2 oz fresh lemon juice

2 tbsp fresh tarragon, chopped

1/2 cup whole grain mustard

1/2 tsp paprika

1/2 tsp pepper

1/4 tsp kosher salt

Directions:

Add all ingredients except chicken to the large bowl and mix well.

Add chicken to the bowl and stir until well coated.

Place the dehydrating tray in a multilevel air fryer basket and place the basket in the instant pot.

Place chicken tenders on dehydrating tray.

Seal pot with air fryer lid and select bake mode, then set the temperature to 380 f and timer for 20 minutes. Turn chicken halfway through.

Serve and enjoy.

Nutrition: Calories 242 Fat 5 g Carbs 1 g Protein 32 g

Creamy Italian chicken

Preparation time: 10 minutes

Cooking time: 10 minutes

Servings: 8

Ingredients:

2 lbs. Chicken breasts, skinless and boneless

1 cup chicken stock

1/4 cup butter

14 oz can cream of chicken soup

8 oz cream cheese

1 tbsp Italian seasoning

Directions:

Add the chicken stock into the inner pot of instant pot duo crisp.

Add cream of chicken soup, Italian seasoning, and butter into the pot and stir well.

Seal the pot with a pressure-cooking lid and cook on high for 10 minutes.

Once done, release pressure using a quick release. Remove lid.

Put and stir the cheese until melted.

Serve and enjoy.

Nutrition: Calories 313 Fat 5g Carbs 7g Protein 52g

Orange curried chicken stir-fry

Preparation time: 10 minutes

Cooking time: 18 minutes

Servings: 4

Ingredients:

1 yellow bell pepper, cut into 1½inch pieces

1 small red onion, sliced

Olive oil for misting

¼ cup chicken stock

2 tablespoons honey

¼ cup of orange juice

1 tablespoon corn starch

3 to 3 teaspoons curry powder

3/4 lb. Chicken thighs boneless

Directions:

Cut the boneless chicken to one inch each piece.

Put the chicken thighs, pepper, and red onion in the instant crisp air fryer basket and mist with olive oil.

Air frying. Lock the air fryer lid. Cook for 1to 14 minutes or until the chicken is cooked to 165°f, shaking the basket halfway through cooking time.

Get the chicken and vegetables from the air fryer basket and set aside.

In a 6inch metal bowl, combine the stock, honey, orange juice, corn starch, curry powder, and mix well. Add the chicken and vegetables, stir, and put the bowl in the basket.

Return the basket to the instant crisp air fryer and cook for 2 minutes.

Remove and stir, then cook for 2 to 3 minutes or until the sauce is thickened and bubbly.

Nutrition: Calories: 437 Fat: 9g Carbs: 54g Protein: 34g

Chicken tikka kebab

Preparation time: 8 hours

Cooking time: 17 minutes

Servings: 4

Ingredients:

1 lb. Chicken thighs boneless skinless, cubed

1 tablespoon oil

1/2 cup red onion, cubed

1/2 cup green bell pepper, cubed

1/2 cup red bell pepper, cubed

Lime wedges to garnish

Onion rounds to garnish

For marinade:

1/2 cup yogurt Greek

3/4 tablespoon ginger, grated

3/4 tablespoon garlic, minced

1 tablespoon lime juice

2 teaspoon red chili powder mild

1/2 teaspoon ground turmeric

1 teaspoon garam masala

1 teaspoon coriander powder

1/2 tablespoon dried fenugreek leaves

1 teaspoon salt

Directions:

Fold in chicken, then mix well to coat and refrigerate for 8 hours.

Add bell pepper, onions, and oil to the marinade and mix well.

Arrange chicken, peppers, and onions on the skewers.

Set the air fryer basket in the instant pot duo.

Put on the air fryer lid and seal it.

Hit the "air fry button" and select 10 minutes of cooking time, then press "start."

Once the instant pot duo beeps and remove its lid.

Flip the skewers and continue air frying for 7 minutes. Serve.

Nutrition: Calories 241 Fat 12g Carbs 5g Protein 28g

Honey cashew butter chicken

Preparation time: 10 minutes

Cooking time: 7 minutes

Servings: 3

Ingredients:

1 lb. Chicken breast, cut into chunks

2 tbsp rice vinegar

2 tbsp honey

2 tbsp coconut aminos

1/4 cup cashew butter

2 garlic cloves, minced

1/4 cup chicken broth

1/2 tbsp sriracha

Directions:

Add chicken into the inner pot of instant pot duo crisp.

In a small bowl, mix cashew butter, garlic, broth, sriracha, vinegar, honey, and coconut aminos and pour over chicken.

Seal the pot with a pressure-cooking lid and cook on high for 7 minutes.

Once done, release pressure using a quick release. Remove lid.

Stir well and serve.

Nutrition: Calories 252 Fat 12g Carbs 24g Protein 16g

Chicken mac and cheese

Preparation time: 10 minutes

Cooking time: 9 minutes

Servings: 6

Ingredients:

2 1/2 cup macaroni

2 cup chicken stock

1 cup cooked chicken, shredded

1 1/4 cup heavy cream

8 tablespoon butter

2 2/3 cups cheddar cheese, shredded

1/3 cup parmesan cheese, shredded

1 bag Ritz crackers

1/4 teaspoon garlic powder

Salt and pepper to taste

Directions:

Add chicken stock, heavy cream, chicken, 4 tablespoon butter, and macaroni to the instant pot duo.

Put on the pressure-cooking lid and seal it.

Hit the "pressure button" and select 4 minutes of cooking time, then press "start."

Crush the crackers and mix them well with tablespoons melted butter.

Once the instant pot duo beeps, do a quick release and remove its lid.

Put on the air fryer lid and seal it.

Hit the "air fryer button" and select 5 minutes of cooking time, then press "start."

Once the instant pot duo beeps, remove its lid. Serve.

Nutrition: Calories 366 Fat 5g Carbs 35g Protein 41g

Maple mustard glazed turkey

Preparation time: 10 minutes

Cooking time: 25 minutes

Servings: 4

Ingredients:

1 turkey breast (about 1½2 lbs.

1 tbsp olive oil

1/4 tsp paprika

1/2 tsp thyme

1/8 tsp dry mustard

1/4 tsp garlic powder

1/2 tsp salt

1/4 tsp freshly ground black pepper

1 tbsp maple syrup

1 tbsp Dijon mustard

1 tbsp unsalted butter, melted

Directions:

Preheat the air fryer to 350°F.

Combine paprika, olive oil, thyme, dry mustard, garlic powder, salt, and freshly ground black pepper in a bowl.

Massage turkey breast with the oil mixture.

Put the turkey in the fryer basket. Cook for 15 minutes.

Once done, turn the turkey breast using tongs and cook for 10 minutes more.

Using a separate bowl, mix the maple syrup, Dijon mustard, and unsalted butter.

Turn the turkey breast and brush the glaze all over the turkey breast.

Cook for 3 minutes more.

Transfer to a serving plate and enjoy!

Nutrition: Calories: 350 Fat: 6g Carbs: 33g Protein: 40g

Turkey and vegetables kabobs

Preparation time: 15 minutes

Cooking time: 20 minutes

Servings: 4

Ingredients:

1/4 cup of soy sauce

1 tbsp honey

2 garlic cloves, minced

1 lb. Boneless skinless turkey breast tenderloins, cut into large chunks

1 large zucchini, cut into chunks

1 yellow bell pepper, chunks

1 red onion, cut into large chunks

1 cup cherry tomatoes

Cooking or olive oil spray

Directions:

Rinse skewers in water for at 30 minutes if using wooden ones.

Preheat the air fryer to 350°F.

Place turkey, zucchini, bell pepper, onion, and tomatoes in a large bowl.

Using a small mixing bowl, combine soy sauce, honey, garlic, and rosemary. Mix well.

Pour prepared sauce over turkey and vegetables and toss to coat well.

Thread the turkey and vegetables onto skewers.

Transfer to the air fryer and spray with cooking spray.

Cook for 15 minutes, flipping once halfway through.

Transfer to the serving plates.

Serve and enjoy!

Nutrition: Calories: 405 Fat: 19g Carbs: 60g Protein: 7g;

Turkey meatloaf

Preparation time: 15 minutes

Cooking time: 25 minutes

Servings: 4

Ingredients:

1 lb. 99% lean ground turkey

1/2 cup breadcrumbs

1 large egg, beaten

1 tbsp tomato paste

1/3 cup of frozen corn

1/4 cup onion, minced

1/4 cup red bell pepper, chopped

1/4 cup scallions, chopped

1 garlic clove, minced

2 tbsp fresh cilantro, chopped

1 tsp salt

1/2 tsp ground cumin

1/4 tsp chili powder

Olive oil spray

2 tbsp ketchup

1 tsp Worcestershire sauce

1 tsp honey

Directions:

Coat the inside of a loaf pan that fits in your air fryer with cooking spray or oil. Set aside.

Preheat the air fryer to 350°F.

Prepare the turkey, breadcrumbs, egg, tomato paste, corn, onion, bell pepper scallions, garlic and fresh cilantro in large mixing bowl.

Season with salt, ground cumin, chili powder and gently mix until just combined.

Place in the prepared loaf pan.

Using a separate bowl, mix ketchup, Worcestershire sauce and honey.

Brush the meatloaves with the ketchup mixture.

Transfer the meatloaf to the air fryer and cook for 20 minutes.

Let cool for 10 minutes before slicing.

Transfer to a serving plate and enjoy!

Nutrition: Calories: 297 Fat: 19g Carbs: 6g Protein: 25g

Turkey cordon bleu

Preparation time: 15 minutes

Cooking time: 20 minutes

Servings: 4

Ingredients:

1 lb. Turkey breast

1 tsp salt

1/4 tsp thyme, dried

1/4 tsp freshly ground black pepper

1 tbsp cream cheese

4 slices ham

4 slices swiss cheese

1 egg, beaten

1/4 cup all-purpose flour

1 cup breadcrumbs

Directions:

Preheat the air fryer to 360°F.

Slice turkey breast into four equal pieces.

Pound each piece slightly with a rolling pin or the smooth side of a meat mallet or heavy skillet until they are about ½inch thick.

Season with salt, thyme, and pepper.

Lay out cream cheese evenly over one side of each piece of meat.

Top with ham slices and swiss cheese.

Roll the breast and secure with toothpicks.

Whisk egg in a small bowl.

Place flour on a shallow plate.

Spread breadcrumbs in a bowl.

Coat the cordon bleu with the flour and then dip in egg.

Sprinkle with breadcrumbs and place in the greased air fryer basket.

Cook for 20 minutes, turning once halfway through.

Transfer to a serving plate and remove toothpicks.

Serve and enjoy!

Nutrition: Calories: 208 Fat: 6g Carbs: 11g Protein: 26g;

Spicy Chicken Tenders with Aioli Sauce

Preparation Time: 10 minutes

Cooking Time: 12 minutes

Servings: 4

Ingredients:

3 chicken breasts, skinless, cut into strips

4 tbsp olive oil

1 cup breadcrumbs

Salt and black pepper to taste

½ tbsp garlic powder

½ tbsp ground chili

½ cup mayonnaise

2 tbsp olive oil

½ tbsp ground chili

Directions:

Mix breadcrumbs, salt, pepper, garlic powder and chili, and spread onto a plate. Spray the chicken with oil. Roll the strips in the breadcrumb mixture until well coated. Spray with a little bit of oil.

Arrange an even layer of strips into your air fryer and cook for 6 minutes at 360 F, turning once halfway through. To prepare the hot aioli: combine mayo with oil and ground chili. Serve hot.

Nutrition: Calories: 490 Fat: 21g Carbs: 34g Protein: 39g

Marinara Sauce Cheese Chicken

Preparation Time: 10 minutes

Cooking time: 15 minutes

Servings: 2

Ingredients:

2 chicken breasts, skinless, beaten, ½-inch thick

1 egg, beaten

½ cup breadcrumbs

A pinch of salt and black pepper

2 tbsp marinara sauce

2 tbsp Grana Padano cheese, grated

2 slices mozzarella cheese

Directions:

Dip the breasts into the egg, then into the crumbs and arrange in the fryer; cook for 5 minutes at 400 F.

Then, turn over and drizzle with marinara sauce, Grana Padano and mozzarella.

Cook for 5 more minutes at 400 F.

Nutrition: Calories: 265 Fat: 10g Carbs: 10g Protein: 32g

Honey Thighs with Garlic

Preparation Time: 10 minutes

Cooking time: 30 minutes

Servings: 4

Ingredients:

4 thighs, skin-on

3 tbsp honey

2 tbsp Dijon mustard

½ tbsp garlic powder

Salt and black pepper to taste

Directions:

In a bowl, mix honey, mustard, garlic, salt, and black pepper.

Coat the thighs in the mixture and arrange them in your air fryer.

Cook for 16 minutes at 400 F, turning once halfway through.

Nutrition: Calories: 294 Fat: 7g Carbs: 19g Protein: 34g

Buttery Chicken with Monterrey Jack Cheese

Preparation Time: 10 minutes

Cooking time: 15 minutes

Servings: 4

Ingredients:

½ cup Italian breadcrumbs

2 tbsp grated Parmesan cheese

1 tbsp butter, melted

4 chicken thighs

½ cup marinara sauce

½ cup shredded Monterrey Jack cheese

Directions:

Spray the air fryer basket with cooking spray. In a bowl, mix the crumbs and Parmesan cheese. Pour the butter into another bowl. Brush the thighs with butter. Dip each one into the crumbs mixture, until well-coated.

Arrange two chicken thighs in the air fryer, and lightly spray with cooking oil.

Cook for 5 minutes at 380 F. Flip over, top with a few tbsp marinara sauce and shredded Monterrey Jack cheese. Cook until no longer pink in the center, for 4 minutes. Repeat with the remaining thighs.

Nutrition: Calories: 290 Fat: 11g Carbs: 36g Protein: 14g

Chicken Breasts with Rosemary

Preparation Time: 10minutes

Cooking time: 20 minutes

Servings: 2

Ingredients:

2 tbsp Dijon mustard

1 tbsp maple syrup

2 tsp minced fresh rosemary

¼ tsp salt

⅛ tsp black pepper

2 chicken breasts, boneless, skinless

Directions:

In a bowl, mix mustard, maple syrup, rosemary, salt, and pepper. Rub mixture onto chicken breasts.

Spray generously the air fryer basket generously with cooking spray.

Arrange the breasts inside and cook for 20 minutes, turning once halfway through.

Nutrition: Calories: 183 Fat: 8g Carbs: 1g Protein: 23g

Thyme Whole Chicken with Pancetta and Lemon

Preparation Time: 15 minutes

Cooking time: 30 minutes

Servings: 4

Ingredients:

1 small whole chicken

1 lemon

4 slices pancetta, roughly chopped

1 onion, chopped

1 sprig fresh thyme

Olive oil

Salt and black pepper

Directions:

In a bowl, mix pancetta, onion, thyme, salt, and black pepper. Pat dry the chicken with a dry paper towel. Insert the pancetta mixture into chicken's cavity and press tight.

Put in the whole lemon and rub the top and sides of the chicken with salt and black pepper. Spray the air fryer's basket with olive oil and arrange the chicken inside.

Cook for 30 minutes on 400 F, turning once halfway through.

Nutrition: Calories: 383 Fat: 16g Carbs: 1g Protein: 55g

Creamy Chicken Nuggets

Preparation Time: 5 minutes

Cooking time: 10 minutes

Servings: 4

Ingredients:

2 chicken breasts, skinless, boneless, cut into nuggets

4 tbsp sour cream

½ cup breadcrumbs

½ tbsp garlic powder

½ tsp cayenne pepper

Salt and black pepper to taste

Directions:

In a bowl, add sour cream and place the chicken. Stir well.

Mix the breadcrumbs, garlic, cayenne, salt, and black pepper and scatter onto a plate.

Roll up the chicken in the breadcrumbs to coat well.

Grease the air with oil. Arrange the nuggets in an even layer and cook for 10 minutes on 360 F, turning once halfway through cooking.

Nutrition: Calories: 215 Fat: 13g Carbs: 10g Protein: 13g

Herby Stuffed Chicken

Preparation Time: 15 minutes

Cooking time: 50 minutes

Servings: 2

Ingredients:

1 small chicken

1 ½ tbsp olive oil

Salt and black pepper to taste to season

1 cup breadcrumbs

⅓ cup chopped sage

⅓ cup chopped thyme

2 cloves garlic, crushed

1 brown onion, chopped

3 tbsp butter

2 eggs, beaten

Directions:

Rinse the chicken gently, pat dry with a paper towel and remove any excess fat with a knife; set aside. On a stove top, place a pan. Add the butter, garlic and onion and sauté to brown. Add the eggs, sage, thyme, pepper, and salt.

Mix well. Cook for 20 seconds and turn the heat off. Stuff the chicken with the mixture into the cavity. Then, tie the legs of the spatchcock with a butcher's twine and brush with olive oil. Rub the top and sides of the chicken generously with salt and pepper. Preheat the Air Fryer to 390 F.

Place the spatchcock into the fryer basket and roast for 25 minutes. Turn the chicken over and continue cooking for 10-15 minutes more; check throughout the cooking time to ensure it doesn't dry or overcooks. Remove onto a chopping board and wrap it with aluminum foil; let rest for 10 minutes. Serve with a side of steamed broccoli.

Nutrition: Calories: 185 Fat: 8g Carbs: 4g Protein: 17g

Chili Chicken Wings

Preparation Time: 16 hours

Cooking time: 16 minutes

Servings: 4

Ingredients:

2 lb. chicken wings

1 tbsp olive oil

3 cloves garlic, minced

1 tbsp chili powder

½ tbsp cinnamon powder

½ tsp allspice

1 habanero pepper, seeded

1 tbsp soy sauce

½ tbsp white pepper

¼ cup red wine vinegar

3 tbsp lime juice

2 Scallions, chopped

½ tbsp grated ginger

½ tbsp chopped fresh thyme

⅓ tbsp sugar

½ tbsp salt

Directions:

In a bowl, add the olive oil, soy sauce, garlic, habanero pepper, allspice, cinnamon powder, cayenne pepper, white pepper, salt, sugar, thyme, ginger, scallions, lime juice, and red wine vinegar; mix well.

Add the chicken wings to the marinade mixture and coat it well with the mixture. Cover the bowl with cling film and refrigerate the chicken to marinate for 16 hours. Preheat the Air Fryer to 400 F. Remove the chicken from the fridge, drain all the liquid, and pat each wing dry using a paper towel.

Place half of the wings in the basket and cook for 16 minutes. Shake halfway through. Remove onto a serving platter and repeat the cooking process for the remaining wings. Serve with blue cheese dip or ranch dressing.

Nutrition: Calories: 191 Fat: 9g Carbs: 13g Protein: 0g

Spice and Juicy Chicken Breasts

Preparation Time: 10 minutes

Cooking time: 25 minutes

Servings: 3

Ingredients:

2 chicken breasts

Salt and black pepper to taste

1 cup flour

3 eggs

½ cup apple cider vinegar

½ tbsp ginger paste

½ tbsp garlic paste

1 tbsp sugar

2 red chilies, minced

2 tbsp tomato puree

1 red pepper

1 green pepper

1 tbsp paprika

4 tbsp water

Directions:

Preheat the Air Fryer to 350 F. Put the chicken breasts on a clean flat surface. Cut them in cubes. Pour the flour in a bowl, crack the eggs in, add the salt and pepper; whisk. Put the chicken in the flour mixture; mix to coat.

Place the chicken in the fryer's basket, spray with cooking spray, and fry for 8 minutes. Pull out the fryer basket, shake to toss, and spray again with cooking spray. Keep cooking for 7 minutes or until golden and crispy.

Remove the chicken to a plate. Put the red, yellow, and green peppers on a chopping board. Using a knife, cut open and deseed them; cut the flesh in long strips. In a bowl, add the water, apple cider vinegar, sugar, ginger and garlic puree, red chili, tomato puree, and smoked paprika; mix with a fork.

Place a skillet over medium heat on a stovetop and spray with cooking spray. Add the chicken and pepper strips. Stir and cook until the peppers are sweaty but still crunchy. Pour the chili mixture on the chicken, stir, and bring to simmer for 10 minutes; turn off the heat. Dish the chicken chili sauce into a serving bowl and serve.

Nutrition: Calories: 173 Fat: 2g Carbs: 9g Protein: 29g

Chicken Kabobs with Garlic Sauce

Preparation Time: 10 minutes

Cooking time: 20 minutes

Servings: 3

Ingredients:

3 chicken breasts

Salt to season

1 tbsp chili powder

¼ cup maple syrup

½ cup soy sauce

2 red peppers

1 green pepper

7 mushrooms

2 tbsp sesame seeds

1 garlic clove

2 tbsp olive oil

Zest and juice from 1 lime

A pinch of salt

¼ cup fresh parsley, chopped

Directions:

Put the chicken breasts on a clean flat surface and cut them in 2-inch cubes with a knife. Add them to a bowl, along with the chili powder, salt, maple syrup, soy sauce, sesame seeds, and spray them with cooking spray. Toss to coat and set aside. Place the peppers on the chopping board. Use a knife to open, deseed and cut in cubes.

Likewise, cut the mushrooms in halves. Start stacking up the Ingredients: - stick 1 red pepper, then green, a chicken cube, and a mushroom half. Repeat the arrangement until the skewer is full. Repeat the process until all the ingredients are used. Preheat the Air Fryer to 330 F.

Brush the kabobs with soy sauce mixture and place them into the fryer basket. Grease with cooking spray and grill for 20 minutes; flip halfway through.

Meanwhile, mix all salsa Verde Ingredients: in your food processor and blend until you obtain a chunky paste. Remove the kabobs when ready and serve with a side of salsa Verde.

Nutrition: Calories: 250 Fat: 5g Carbs: 5g Protein: 30g

Zucchini Stuffed Lemony Chicken

Preparation Time: 20 minutes

Cooking time: 2 hours

Servings: 6

Ingredients:

1 whole chicken, 3 lb.

2 red and peeled onions

2 tbsp olive oil

2 apricots

1 zucchini

1 apple

2 cloves finely chopped garlic

Fresh chopped thyme

Salt and black pepper to taste

5 oz honey

juice from 1 lemon

2 tbsp olive oil

Salt and black pepper to taste

Directions:

For the stuffing, chop all Ingredients: into tiny pieces. Transfer to a large bowl and add the olive oil. Season with salt and black pepper. Fill the cavity of the chicken with the stuffing, without packing it tightly.

Place the chicken in the Air Fryer and cook for 35 minutes at 340 F. Warm the honey and the lemon juice in a large pan; season with salt and pepper. Reduce the temperature of the Air Fryer to 320 F.

Brush the chicken with some of the honey-lemon marinade and return it to the fryer. Cook for another 70 minutes; brush the chicken every 20-25 minutes with the marinade. Garnish with parsley and serve with potatoes.

Nutrition: Calories: 179 Fat: 4g Carbs: 21g Protein: 19g

Preparation Time: 2 hours

Cooking time: 25 minutes

Servings: 4

Ingredients:

1 lb. mini drumsticks

3 tbsp butter

3 tbsp paprika

2 tbsp powdered cumin

¼ cup hot sauce

1 tbsp maple syrup

2 tbsp onion powder

2 tbsp garlic powder

½ cup mayonnaise

1 cup crumbled blue cheese

1 cup sour cream

1 ½ tbsp garlic powder

1 ½ tbsp onion powder

Salt and black pepper to taste

1 ½ tbsp cayenne pepper

1 ½ tbsp white wine vinegar

2 tbsp buttermilk

1 ½ Worcestershire sauce

Directions:

Start with the drumstick sauce; place a pan over medium heat on a stove top. Melt the butter, and add the hot sauce, paprika, garlic, onion, maple syrup, and cumin; mix well. Cook the mixture for 5 minutes or until the sauce reduces. Turn off the heat and let cool. Put the drumsticks in a bowl, pour half of the sauce over, and mix it.

Save the remaining sauce for serving. Refrigerate the drumsticks for 2 hours. Meanwhile, make the blue cheese sauce: in a jug, add the sour cream, blue cheese, mayonnaise, garlic powder, onion powder, buttermilk, cayenne pepper, vinegar, Worcestershire sauce, pepper, and salt. Using a stick blender, blend the Ingredients: until they are well mixed with no large lumps. Adjust the salt and pepper taste as desired. Preheat the Air Fryer to 350 F.

Remove the drumsticks from the fridge and place them in the fryer basket; cook for 15 minutes. Turn the drumsticks with tongs every 5 minutes to ensure that they are evenly cooked. Remove the drumsticks to a serving bowl and pour the remaining sauce over. Serve with the blue cheese sauce and a side of celery sticks.

Nutrition: Calories: 210 Fat: 13g Carbs: 1g Protein: 22g

Chili Lime Chicken Lollipop

Preparation Time: 15 minutes

Cooking time: 10 minutes

Servings: 3

Ingredients:

1 lb. mini chicken drumsticks

½ tbsp soy sauce

1 tbsp lime juice

Salt and black pepper to taste

1 tbsp corn starch

½ tbsp minced garlic

½ tbsp chili powder

½ tbsp chopped cilantro

½ tbsp garlic-ginger paste

1 tbsp vinegar

1 tbsp chili paste

½ tbsp beaten egg

1 tbsp paprika

1 tbsp flour

2 tbsp maple syrup

Directions:

Mix garlic ginger paste, chili powder, maple syrup, paprika powder, chopped coriander, plain vinegar, egg, garlic, and salt, in a bowl.

Add the chicken drumsticks and toss to coat; Stir in corn starch, flour, and lime juice.

Preheat the Air Fryer to 350 F. Remove each drumstick, shake off the excess marinade, and place in a single layer in the basket; cook for 5 minutes.

Slide out the basket, spray the chicken with cooking spray and continue to cook for 5 minutes. Remove onto a serving platter and serve with tomato dip and a side of steamed asparagus.

Nutrition: Calories: 150 Fat: 5g Carbs: 1g Protein: 25g

Almond Turkey with Lemon and Eggs

Preparation Time: 15 minutes

Cooking time: 35 minutes

Servings: 3

Ingredients:

1 lb. turkey breasts

Salt and black pepper to taste to season

¼ cup chicken soup cream

¼ cup mayonnaise

2 tbsp lemon juice

¼ cup slivered almonds, chopped

¼ cup breadcrumbs

2 tbsp chopped green onion

2 tbsp chopped pimentos

2 Boiled eggs, chopped

½ cup diced celery

Directions:

Preheat the Air Fryer to 390 F. Place the turkey breasts on a clean flat surface and season with salt and pepper.

Grease with cooking spray and place them in the fryer's basket; cook for 13 minutes. Remove turkey back onto the chopping board, let cool, and cut into dices. In a bowl, add the celery, chopped eggs, pimentos, green onions, slivered almonds, lemon juice, mayonnaise, diced turkey, and chicken soup cream and mix well.

Grease a 5 X 5 inches casserole dish with cooking spray, scoop the turkey mixture into the bowl, sprinkle the breadcrumbs on it, and spray with cooking spray. Put the dish in the fryer basket and bake the Ingredients: at 390 F for 20 minutes. Remove and serve with a side of steamed asparagus.

Nutrition: Calories: 214 Fat: 6g Carbs: 18g Protein: 21g

Party Chicken Wings with Sesame

Preparation Time: 10 minutes

Cooking time: 12 minutes

Servings: 4

Ingredients:

1 lb. chicken wings

2 tbsp sesame oil

2 tbsp maple syrup

Salt and black pepper

3 tbsp sesame seeds

Directions:

In a bowl, add wings, oil, maple syrup, salt and pepper, and stir to coat well.

In another bowl, add the sesame seeds and roll the wings in the seeds to coat thoroughly.

Arrange the wings in an even layer inside your air fryer and cook for 12 minutes on 360 F, turning once halfway through.

Buttermilk Chicken Bites

Preparation Time: 10 minutes

Cooking time: 12 minutes

Servings: 4

Ingredients:

2 chicken breasts, skinless, cut into 2 pieces each

1 egg, beaten

¼ cup buttermilk

1 cup corn flakes, crushed

Salt and black pepper to taste

Directions:

In a bowl, whisk egg and buttermilk. Add in chicken pieces and stir to coat.

In a plate, spread the cornflakes out and mix with salt and pepper. Coat the chicken pieces in the cornflakes. Spray the air fryer with cooking spray.

Arrange the chicken in an even layer in the air fryer; cook for 12 minutes at 360 F, turning once halfway through.

Nutrition: Calories: 230 Fat: 9g Carbs: 20g Protein: 18g

Savory Chicken Burgers

Preparation Time: 10 minutes

Cooking time: 10 minutes

Servings: 4

Ingredients:

1 lb. ground chicken

½ onion, chopped

2 garlic cloves, chopped

1 egg, beaten

½ cup breadcrumbs

½ tbsp ground cumin

½ tbsp paprika

½ tbsp cilantro seeds, crushed

Salt and black pepper to taste

Directions:

In a bowl, mix chicken, onion, garlic, egg, breadcrumbs, cumin, paprika, cilantro, salt, and black pepper, with hands; shape into 4 patties.

Grease the air fryer with oil and arrange the patties inside. Do not layer them. Cook in batches if needed.

Cook for 10 minutes at 380 F, turning once halfway through.

Nutrition: Calories: 250 Fat: 13g Carbs: 5g Protein: 26g

Creamy Chicken with Prosciutto

Preparation Time: 10 minutes

Cooking time: 15 minutes

Servings: 2

Ingredients:

2 chicken breasts

1 tbsp olive oil

Salt and black pepper to taste to season

1 cup semi-dried tomatoes, sliced

½ cup brie cheese, halved

4 slices thin prosciutto

Directions:

Preheat the Air Fryer to 365 F. Put the chicken on a chopping board and cut a small incision deep enough to make stuffing on both. Insert one slice of cheese and 4 to 5 tomato slices into each chicken.

Lay the prosciutto on the chopping board. Put the chicken on one side and roll the prosciutto over the chicken making sure that both ends of the prosciutto meet under the chicken.

Drizzle olive oil and sprinkle with salt and pepper. Place the chicken in the basket and cook for 10 minutes. Turn the breasts over and cook for another 5 minutes. Slice each chicken breast in half and serve with tomato salad.

Nutrition: Calories: 414 Fat: 16g Carbs: 16g Protein: 41g

Conclusion

The air fryer works great for foods like roasted vegetables, especially roasted garlic, bacon, whole chicken, wings, eggs, meat, and fish. Most air fryers come with timers and temperature adjustments to make for more precise cooking. There is an opening at the top that takes in air, heated up by the heating rings, and subsequently blown over the food, thereby efficiently cooking them. A cooking basket also sits on top of a drip tray inside which the food is cooked. This basket needs to be shaken frequently to ensure even mixing of oil and a better cooking result. While most models have agitators that initiate this shaking at regular intervals, most others do not, and the shaking should be done manually.

CPSIA information can be obtained
at www.ICGtesting.com
Printed in the USA
LVHW081623100521
687014LV00011B/853